MOMStories

Minute Meditations for Mothers

Vickie LoPiccolo Jennett

with meditation questions by Paula Hagen, OSB

Resource Publications, Inc.
San Jose, California

Reprint Department
Resource Publications, Inc.
160 E. Virginia Street #290
San Jose, CA 95112-5876
(408) 286-8505 voice
(408) 287-8748 fax

Library of Congress Cataloging-in-Publication Data
Jennett, Vickie LoPiccolo, 1955–
    MOMStories: minute meditations for mothers / Vickie LoPiccolo Jennett; with meditation questions by Paula Hagen.
        p.   cm.
    Includes indexes.
    ISBN 0-89390-474-0 (pbk.)
        1. Mothers—Religious life. 2. Motherhood—Religious aspects—Christianity—Meditations. I. Title: MOM stories. II. Hagen, Paula, 1937– III. Title.
    BV4529.18 .J46 1999
    242'.6431—dc21   99-051609

Printed in the United States of America
99 00 01 02 03 | 5 4 3 2 1

Editor: Nick Wagner
Production manager: Elizabeth J. Asborno
Production assistant: Kathi Drolet
Cover design: Mike Sagara

About the cover: Needlework designer Maureen Appleton graciously offered an adaptation of her original design, "Bless me Lord," to accompany the second book in the MOMStories series. The creator of more than 200 original counted thread works of art, Maureen is known for the unique detail and heirloom quality of her sampler and botanical designs. Over the years, Maureen's daughter Andrea has lovingly supported her mother's business, *The Heart's Content,* 4440 Indian Trail, Green Bay, WI 54313.

This book is dedicated to the memory of all moms,
but especially to these women whose wisdom
and legacy of love extend
far beyond their years on this earth:

Lilian Okner Feinberg, 1917–1998
Mary Fernandez Lester, 1956–1996
Rose Maida Palen, 1933–1998
Joanne McKeever Torzala, 1955–1999

Contents

Don't skip this preface!

I wasn't the clever one who came up with the subtitle for this MOMStories. But, when I heard it, I was pleased—likely because minute doses of wisdom, quiet time, and meditation are all I have (or make) time for in a day. The old "hurrieder I go behinder I get" adage aptly characterizes the life I have chosen to lead—a crazy but good life chock-full of miles on the road, smiles on our faces, and love in our hearts. I rarely sit still, but when I do, my fingers are tapping away at the keyboard or stitching away on an ongoing cross-stitch project.

In those very rare moments when even my fingers lie still, my mind wanders to places of peace and relative quiet, slightly aware of soothing sounds coming either from the chirping birds in our backyard or from instrumentals on the CD player. A slight breeze accompanies the sun's rays while God's splendid wisdom fills my mind. I sometimes even yearn to lead the serene, orderly life depicted in an Ellen Stouffer painting. I have never met or even spoken to this Wabash, Indiana, artist. However, for years, her calendars have spoken to me daily of sheep-laden meadows, bountiful harvest baskets, and peaceful tables set for tea. She seems to have found that perfect balance of peace and harmony with herself, her environment, and her God.

It is my fondest hope that each of you finds a similar comfort and joy in the MOMStories presented here. After all, they are your stories. They come from far and wide, speaking of miracles and memories, joy and tragedy. Combining these stories with Scripture reminds us that our lives are holy, that our actions and words are of God. Each time I read Scripture written thousands of years ago, I marvel that we're still striving to get the message. After all these years, only a very few, very holy folks have mastered the Master's instructions.

I suppose what makes me smile is that it's okay we're still grappling with trying to get the message. God's plan is to give us the gifts and the grace, then let us muddle through making choices and plans based on the Good News. In God's infinite wisdom, we are blessed with forgiveness and the courage to go on. He gives us one another along the journey—to support, encourage, listen, advise. That's the whole idea behind MOMStories.

Telling Our Stories

One especially wise mom, Trish Hoyt, shared these words with us in *Instant Inspiration for Mothers*. Her words are simple and straightforward, worth repeating and remembering:

> "Once upon a time...," my mother began so many times. It is to her that I attribute my love of storytelling. To this day, I can feel her words soothing the angst of our young hearts and fueling our wildest, most enchanted dreams. She understood that stories feed the soul and speak to our imagination. The best of stories help us aspire to great things or help us name ourselves into a new way of being. We are blessed that our Christian tradition offers us a wealth of biblical stories. These are some of the stories I tell my children, along with stories of their birth, their beginnings, their early days. I tell them of their importance in my life. And I tell them fictional stories of animals and heroes, dreamers and lost folk—anything and everything that touches the heart. In time I will tell my children stories of zany relatives, stories of teen and adult struggles, stories of hopes dashed and dreams realized. Meanwhile, I invite listeners to step into my stories, praying the listeners will walk with me a while, not judging or analyzing my stories but simply *being there* with me. This is what the listener does, what a soulmate does, what a parent does. After all, this is what our God does. How can we do less?

With Gratitude

Thanks to all the women who contributed to MOMStories. Your comments in classes, retreats, workshops, MOMS groups and newsletters are the basis for these inspiring glimpses at God's presence in our lives. Your e-mail messages, faxes, and letters are encouraging and inspiring. Thanks especially to these women for their wit, wisdom, support, and stories:

Donna Cachero	Jennifer Henderson
Janice C. Capone	Janie Jasin
Mary Ann Caroline	Anne Jones
Monica Charnell	Jana Kotsur
Eunice Mello Cheshire	Theresa McCutchan
Kathe Collins	MOMS Regional Coordinators
Valerie Conzett	Margie Plunkett
Jenny Cook	Pat Richards
Heather Darrow	Nancee Ryan
Terri Farley	Donna M. Simons
Joan Feraro	Joan Soller
Kathy Gowen	Rebecca Stephensen
Brenda Clark Hamilton	Stacy M. Stroup
Yasmin Hauke	Barbara Feenstra
Jeanne Hayes	Liz Williams
Roberta Hemphill	Marian Wittman

Acknowledgments

The Scripture quotations contained herein are from the New Revised Standard Version of the Bible, Catholic Edition, copyrighted 1993, by the Division of Christian Education of the National Council of the Churches of Christ in the United States of America, and are used by permission. All rights reserved.

The "Group Rules for Ongoing Groups," page 62, is reprinted from *MOMS: Developing a Ministry* by Paula Hagen and Patricia Hoyt, © 1995 Resource Publications Inc., and is used with permission. All rights reserved.

More MOMStories?

You are invited to continue telling and sending your MOMStories to viclj@worldnet.att.net or faxing them to (480) 895-2214.

"I give thanks to my God always for you because of the grace of God that has been given you in Christ Jesus, for in every way you have been enriched in him, in speech and knowledge of every kind…."
1 Corinthians 1:4–5

When liabilities turn to friendships

Having a younger sibling can be an incredible burden. I know. I'm the big sister. I'm also a mother who just witnessed the sweet transition when little brother converts from liability to friend. Sad to say, for my sister and me this transition came about much later in life. Over the years, the three-year age difference between my boys has made for interesting playground routs and dinner table conversations. It also has created minor skirmishes and conflicts that typically arise when older brother thinks he's too cool, knows it all. Likewise, younger brother sometimes overrates the humor of his antics or pesters the heck out of big brother. Thankfully, though, the balancing act never has gotten out of hand. The big breakthrough came at ages fourteen and seventeen. Younger brother could finally understand big brother's seemingly endless primping and hours on the phone. Older brother responded with a bit more tolerance for younger brother. What sealed their relationship was younger brother's new puppy, a cute fur ball that became an instant hit with both boys—not to mention that the pooch was the perfect ploy for older brother to get his latest love interest to visit. Big brother needed his friend—his little brother.

For Meditation
- How have God's grace and love come to me through a difficult relationship?
- What do I do that enriches the lives of those around me?
- As an adult, how have I learned to be more grateful to God?

My Thoughts

Comfort, O comfort my people,
says your God. / Isaiah 40:1

Comfort touch

The nighttime silence was deafening. The dimly lit church was
the sight of an all-night open casket vigil for an eighteen-month-old
who died of a rare disease. Sometime around 11 P.M., my
son-in-law walked in with his eight-year-old daughter. She sat
silently for a while; then she got up and gently stroked the
angelic face in the casket. My granddaughter was relaxed, as if
she were stroking her favorite kitten. My heart was about to
burst with the pride and the joy of grandmotherhood. All of our
talks about life, death, God, and love were represented in this
tender moment. She had naturally grasped an understanding of
the fragility of life. With God's grace, her parents and I had
succeeded in helping her accept death as part of God's plan.
In her little heart and little mind, she did not recall a similar
situation five years earlier when she asked why her grandfather
was so cold and so still. Perhaps tucked away somewhere in her
subconscious mind, this earlier experience helped provide the
comfort and courage she needed to face sorrow and death.

For Meditation
• Where does my mind wander in the silence of the night?
• When my anguish seems unbearable, how does God comfort
  me? Do I reach out to comfort those who are facing painful
  times?
• What can I learn of comfort from little children?

My Thoughts

Rejoice always, pray without ceasing, give thanks in all circumstances; for this is the will of God in Christ Jesus for you.
1 Thessalonians 5:16

Oops!

One night as I was tucking my then-three-year-old daughter into bed, we were saying the Lord's Prayer together when a few of her words got mixed up. What was supposed to be "as we forgive those who trespass against us" became "as we forgive those who passed gas against us"!

She caught herself and looked up at me with her brown eyes as large as saucers and very innocently asked, "That's not how it goes, is it?"

We both laughed until we cried and talked about how growing up with three brothers could actually lead one to believe that passing gas is something for which forgiveness is needed. How good it feels to have those belly-laughs from such unexpected places. How wonderful to have the freedom to laugh while we pray. It was right then and there that I asked the Lord to help me not to take myself (or my kids) too seriously. I also thanked God for reminding me that prayer time can (and should) include a few laughs.

For Meditation
- How does laughter enrich my prayer life? My life in general?
- When does taking myself too seriously get in the way of enjoying life, of being spontaneously open to God's grace?
- How do I reconcile my mistakes with myself?

My Thoughts

I will sing of your steadfast love, O LORD, forever;
  with my mouth I will proclaim your faithfulness to all generations.
Psalm 89:1

Lest we forget

How easily our children forget that we love them every minute of every day. As toddlers, we warn them of impending danger or guide them from harm's way. They mistake our loving concern for anger. Throughout their school years, we remind them to do their homework, clean their rooms, and be nice to their siblings. In their minds, our words to the wise become meddling messages. Who wants to clean up for dinner when everyone in the neighborhood is playing in the new-fallen snow? Who wants to finish a science project when a friend just called with a movie invite? It's easy to confuse love with authority.

  Then the teenage years arrive and our love is still perceived as meddling, yet it goes on nonetheless—from squabbles with boyfriends to curfews broken, from running out of gas to running into trouble. We stand by our children in good times and in bad, just as God stands by our sides through the ups and downs of life. Like our children, we're sometimes oblivious to that everpresent love. We take for granted the warm embrace that awaits our weary minds and bodies. Every minute of every day, God's love is there, steadfast, even when we do forget.

For Meditation
• In what ways do I "sing of God's steadfast love"?
• What memories do I hold dear from my teenage years? What memories cause me pain?
• How can I be concerned about my family and those I love without becoming a "mother hen"?

My Thoughts

"Do not be afraid; for see—I am bringing you good news of great joy for all the people: to you is born this day in the city of David a Savior, who is the Messiah, the Lord." / Luke 2:10–11

Growing pains

Lord, my eyes fill with stinging tears as I drive by the school where my children spend six or seven hours each day. I know this is all part of their growing up and branching out process. But it seems as if school has snatched my precious twins away from me. Why am I still reacting this way when they have been in first grade now for months? I know they are your children, entrusted to me here on earth.

The simplest things, like a crane lifting up a huge steel beam at a construction site, remind me how much they delight at sharing the simple pleasures of every day. Then I pass the park, missing our frequent trips there—as well as storytime at the library. I miss the little hands that used to cling to the shopping cart for safety as I crossed the parking lot.

These are bittersweet times for me. I'm at a stage in my life once again asking you, "God, what am I going to do with my life?" I pray daily that the Lord will lead me through the open door to what my future holds.

For Meditation
- God lends us his children for a while. How can I accept the fact that they grow up and move on or may be snatched from my grasp at any moment?
- When my fear keeps me from functioning, how can conversation with others help me get another perspective and move forward?
- What gets in the way of my being hopeful and positive, recognizing the Messiah in my life?

My Thoughts

As God's chosen ones, holy and beloved, clothe yourselves with compassion, kindness, humility, meekness, and patience. Bear with one another and, if anyone has a complaint against another, forgive each other; just as the Lord has forgiven you, so you also must forgive. Above all, clothe yourselves with love, which binds everything together in perfect harmony. And let the peace of Christ rule in your hearts.... Colossians 3:12–15

A mother's love

Sometimes what we pray for is answered in ways we never could have imagined.

My oldest son was having some tough times and all I could ask God for during the biting, Midwest winters was that he would be warm and have enough food to survive. Things were not looking good. Then he was sent to prison. I never dreamed that the answer to my prayers would be prison. There he was able to do his drawings to earn money to buy extra rations. There he was warm and had access to good medical treatment. There he had the time to write letters and read books. There he knew he had a place to sleep. There he had the security of knowing his meals would be served three times a day.

Thank you, God, for being imaginative with your answer to my prayers.

For Meditation
- What are some of the unexpected lessons I have learned through prayer and through opening my mind?
- Where do I find compassion, kindness, humility, meekness, and patience in my life?
- Do I see my family as "God's chosen ones, holy and beloved?"

My Thoughts

Then you shall see and be radiant;
  your heart shall thrill and rejoice…. / Isaiah 60:5

Simply sacred

How clearly I remember hearing our pastor say, "Your family life
at home is sacred. Your daily activities are holy." These words,
presented at my son's first communion preparation several years
ago, changed my life.

At first they seemed incredibly frightening. How could my
daily, meaningless drudgery be holy? Laundry? Cooking? Picking
mess after grandiose mess? Then I thought about my yelling and
the many moments of disharmony in our family. What a
frightening thought. How, I wondered, could all of this be holy?
How might Mary or Elizabeth handle similar situations?

Understanding his words didn't come over night. But, over
time, as I thought and prayed about our pastor's words, they
became quite liberating. Eventually, a sense of great love and
warmth filled the spot that had been occupied by fear. As a
mother, my love for my family and our home truly is holy.
The laundry and dishes and help with homework are special acts
of love that do contribute to our sense of home. They aren't
empty, endless tasks that just take up time. Amazing how a few
words gleaned from a sermon could be the impetus for changing
my thought process. It feels good to know that our home life is holy!

For Meditation
- Am I aware of all the simple, ordinary holiness that fills my
  day? How can I become more aware of what is sacred in my life?
- What creates a sense of "home" for me? For my loved ones?
- How do I carry the Eucharist home within me to help my heart
  rejoice all week long? How am I an "Eucharistic person?"

My Thoughts

"May the LORD give strength to his people!
May the LORD bless his people with peace!" / Psalm 29:11

My medal

As a nurse practitioner in a family practice setting, my work requires doing quite a few physical exams and annual gynecological exams. One young woman who came to see me was in generally good health, except she complained of being "bothered" by her swollen abdomen despite having done numerous situps and other exercises. The twenty-eight-year-old nurse, married for three years, had no children. During the exam, it became apparent that not poor muscle tone but a large uterine tumor was responsible for her distended stomach. How could I tell her my suspected diagnosis? I silently asked the Holy Spirit for guidance and the right words. Our discussion led her to see a gynecologist later that day, followed by a hysterectomy for what turned out to be cancer. The outlook, she reports, is promising, although she and her husband never will have children.

When I spoke to her following the surgery, she was in good spirits looking toward a bright future. She told me that when I first saw her in the office, she noticed my Virgin Mary and Christ-child pendant and could focus only on that icon. It is what gave her the strength and serenity that someone was watching over her in this difficult time. She opened my eyes to the values we shared. She now has her own matching medal.

For Meditation
- What can I do to be more thankful for the compassionate medical personnel who serve me and my family?
- How can I deliver even devastating messages with compassion?
- When I need strength and peace, do I immediately think to seek out the Lord?

My Thoughts

Speak, LORD, for your servant is listening. / 1 Samuel 3:9

A listening ear

As a new grandmother of five, I can vividly recall being a new mother of four. How fast the time has passed. Our three oldest children were quite close in age—three born within three years. The middle of the three was noticeably feeling squeezed out one day, lacking the attention lavished on the oldest and on the baby. I had no idea how left out he was feeling until one day when the family was chatting about God and heaven. "When I go to heaven," he announced to his siblings, "I'm going to sleep in God's ear!"

His need to be close to his heavenly Father, so close he would always be heard, made me smile. It also made me realize how comfortable his relationship must have been with God. I was grateful, too, to be nudged into giving him more of my attention, not to mention a listening ear.

For Meditation
• Is it difficult for me to listen when the Lord is speaking? When?
• To whom do I give a great deal of my attention? How do I find balance when dividing my attention? What helps me to slow down and listen?
• What do my loved ones have to do to get my attention?

My thoughts

Make me to know your ways, O LORD;
    teach me your paths.
Lead me in your truth, and teach me…. / Psalm 25:4–5

Shopping cart wisdom

I was trying to mind my own business, really I was, when I overheard a mother questioning something her toddler had just said. Her gentle voice had an incredulous tone, wondering where the curly-headed lad could possibly have heard the phrase in question. "That's not something we call people," she instructed. "We call people by their names. We call them nice things—like pretty or wonderful or silly. We thank people and we hug people, but we don't call them bad names. That was a bad name and I don't want to hear you say it again."

By this time, I was guilty of outright eavesdropping. My heart was filled by this tender teaching moment between mother and son. She had no idea that her simple wisdom was an inspiration to a mother who had been through so many similar situations a dozen years prior. I couldn't remain quiet. I must have sounded like an idiot, approaching a stranger's shopping cart and thanking her for taking the time to seize this teachable moment with her son. "See," she told him, "other people hear what you say, so you want to make sure it's something good."

He smiled at me, and I said, "With a mom like that, you'll grow up to be a great young man." He reached out and hugged his mom. Our eyes filled with tears as we went back to our shopping.

For Meditation
• How do I inspire my family to stay on the path toward heaven?
• Who teaches me God's truths? Where do I find inspiration?
• Do I compliment others sincerely? Do I accept compliments graciously?

My Thoughts

I will raise up for them a prophet like you from among their own people; I will put my words in the mouth of the prophet who shall speak to them everything that I command. / Deuteronomy 18:18

Author unknown

Every now and then, we hear stories that are too good to keep to ourselves. Their origins are questionable. They may even be fiction. It makes no matter, because their messages are potent. By the time these stories make their way to us, the names and facts may have changed a dozen times. They may be abbreviated or exaggerated. The one thing that remains unchanged, however, is their wisdom.

This "legend" involves a child saying his before-meal prayers at a restaurant. His words were straightforward and heartfelt: "God is great, God is good, I want to thank Him for my food, and I want to ask Him for some ice cream, too. And lead us not into temptation with liberty and justice for all."

The laughter from nearby patrons was cut short by one woman's disdain: "That's the problem with kids today. They just don't know how to pray. Can you imagine, asking God for ice cream? Why I never...."

Assuring her son that he had done a terrific job with his prayers, the mother's spirits were bolstered by one man's comments, "I happen to know that God thought yours was a great prayer. In fact," he said glancing at the grouchy woman, "more people should ask for ice cream. It's good for the soul."

For Meditation
• What is good for my soul? Do I make time to nourish my soul?
• Whose words inspire me? Who are today's prophets?
• Do I take time to really listen to my children and their friends? My grandchildren?

My Thoughts

Do not human beings have a hard service on earth,
and are not their days like the days of a laborer?
Like a slave who longs for the shadow,
and like laborers who look for their wages.... / *Job 7:1–2*

Fairness

"Would we appreciate the wonders of God's blessings if they were too easy?"

A friend recently posed that question to me as we discussed her first grandchild's dramatic entry into the world.

It's a question I have asked myself and my children many times over the years as we faced struggles, challenges and difficult decisions. How can we open our eyes to God's great love for us? How can I teach my children to value the spiritual in such a materialistic society? The questions seem overwhelming.

Throughout their growing-up years, my children have repeatedly asked questions regarding those who have vast worldly possessions.

My answers over the years haven't been terrifically inspiring, yet they seemed to satisfy the kids. "This isn't about fairness," I would say. "Count your blessings and don't worry what other people have or don't have. Just be responsible for what you do have. Money isn't everything. Why are so many 'rich' people addicted to drugs, sex, and alcohol? Maybe it's just as hard to be rich as it is to be poor. Only God knows."

For Meditation

- How do I keep a balance of work, play, and prayer in our family life?
- When I share my trials with others, how are my burdens lightened?
- What importance do I attach to money and other material possessions? Do material things control me and my happiness?

My Thoughts

So, whether you eat or drink, or whatever you do, do everything for the glory of God. / 1 Corinthians 10:31

Laugh a while

In college, I had a professor whose area of expertise was humor. Global humor. Those universal foibles and embarrassing little moments that tickle funny bones from Boston to Bali. For years, he had traveled the world gathering examples, jotting down notes, and doing studies. He characterized and categorized all types of humor, ancient and modern, gutter and sophisticated. Some things, he told us, are funny no matter where you are. Other forms of humor are specific to a region or culture. He knew for a fact that laughter *is* the best medicine.

I finished my humor class and sort of forgot about it until I had children. Thank heaven someone had thought to warn me that "bathroom humor" was universal. Otherwise, I would have thought my children were warped. What a blessing to know that humorous moments really do crop up when least expected— even if it happens to be in the midst of an important meeting or twenty minutes into a church service. I was relieved to understand that not all forms of hilarity have the same impact on everyone. Some of the jokes my kids bring home disgust me. (At least they tell me what they're hearing.) But, then again, they think my jokes are corny. God certainly does have a sense of humor. No kidding!

For Meditation
• How can laughter enrich my life and lighten my load?
• When is the time I really enjoyed a good belly-laugh? Who are my laughing friends?
• How can I boost my spirits and the spirits of those around me for the glory of God?

My Thoughts

"...they were all amazed and glorified God, saying, 'We have never seen anything like this!' " / Mark 2:12

Take a look

My grace-filled moments often come courtesy of my children. This Monday morning was like any other Monday morning. I was in a hurry to get my boys to their grandmother's home so I could get to work on time. I saw nothing except the clock on the dashboard and the road ahead. My mind was intently focused on getting to work on time, my brain going full speed, keeping up with the car's racing engine. Suddenly, my thoughts were interrupted by a sweet voice from the back seat.

"Hey, look at the beautiful sky the angels painted for us!"

"Sky," I mused, "I hadn't even noticed the sky."

When I glanced out the window, I beheld one of the most incredible sunrises I had ever seen. The sun was peeking over a hill on the horizon. Colors of orange, yellow, pink, and purple beamed from behind large, puffy, white clouds.

At that moment, I realized that my three-year-old son had one up on me. He knew the most important morning activity was to take notice and appreciate God's works. My son's comment also reminded me that I needed to slow down and do likewise. I need to share more of these "angel-painted morning skies" with my sons. We all need to see more skies like this!

For Meditation
- What step toward peace and tranquility can I take today?
- Who are some peace-filled people I admire? Can I talk with them or read a book they have written?
- How do I thank my children for moments of enlightenment they share with me?

My Thoughts

You yourselves are our letter, written on our hearts, to be known and read by all; and you show that you are a letter of Christ, prepared by us, written not with ink but with the Spirit of the living God, not on tablets of stone but on tablets of human hearts. / 2 Corinthians 3:2–3

Our children

My son stood near the altar with forty-some other confirmation candidates. To my surprise and delight, he came forward to the microphone, letting a church full of family and friends know how much his four-day retreat meant to him. Within minutes, dozens of other teens repeated similar heartfelt testimonies. My own heart jumped for joy as I recognized not one or two but a half-dozen names and faces from a kindergarten catechism class I had led twelve years prior. For more than a decade, these young people had grown and matured, fallen and gotten up. Realizing that they and their families had nurtured their faith relationships brought a smile with warmth that radiated through my very being.

Those little people in a kindergarten class, so curious and energetic, had funneled their energy into the formidable task of walking with Christ as they moved through adolescence and teenage years. Now they were embarking on a new journey. It was as if each one was my own child.

For Meditation
- In what ways have I reached out to nurture faith development in the hearts and minds of the next generation?
- How do I prepare myself each day to face challenges to my faith and belief?
- What changes need to be written on the tablet of my human heart by the "Spirit of the living God?"

My Thoughts

*The Sabbath was made for humankind, and not humankind for the
Sabbath; so the Son of Man is Lord even of the Sabbath.*
Mark 2:27–28

Church bells

The turning point in my family's faith came one Sunday morning
while shopping in a beautiful mountain town. I was pushing my
eighteen month old in a stroller as the sun and wind blended to
create the near-perfect climate when the lovely sound of church
bells filled the air.

As the bells continued, my daughter looked back at me and
asked, "What's that, Mommy, Taco Bells?" After laughing at her
cute question, I realized it also had a very serious side. I had
never taken my daughter to church. Church bells were foreign to
her. She had no idea what church was all about or who God was.

That was six years ago, and we've been faith-filled participants
at our church ever since. I thank God daily for teaching me
through the insight of my daughter. Whenever I hear church
bells, I am gently reminded of this special moment. Their
soothing sound rings true in my heart.

For Meditation
- What are some of the healthy habits I want to strengthen in
  my life? In my family?
- Faith and spiritual development are very personal choices.
  What are my spiritual goals and choices?
- How do I monitor my spiritual progress?

My Thoughts

...therefore teach me wisdom in my secret heart.
Let me hear joy and gladness.... / Psalm 51:6,8

Living in the present

My oldest child, a boy, will be seven in the spring. What will become of this fun-loving, cuddly child? What will the future bring? What is in store along the pathways of his life? My concern often turns to worry when I contemplate the encounters he may face in the years to come. When I hug him close, I can actually feel the young man inside, waiting to emerge. How much longer can we share these mother-son moments? Will he welcome my affection, my love, my smiles and jokes? Will other interests draw him away from us? What a short period of time our children are with us.

It wasn't until I discussed these feelings with other mothers that I realized I was not alone. Many of the "more experienced" mothers suggested that I work at focusing on making every moment count rather than worrying over what will come. Their wisdom, their gift of faith, has helped me to live in the present, to savor the hugs for what they are—a loving bond between mother and son that warms my heart and fuels my soul.

For Meditation
• How do I respond to the things I have to do—the obligations and responsibilities in my life?
• What do I do just for me when I finish all the "things" I am required to do in a day?
• What symbols of faith do I notice surrounding me? Which ones do I pass on to my children? My grandchildren?

My Thoughts

For Christ also suffered for sins once for all, the righteous for the unrighteous, in order to bring you to God. He was put to death in the flesh, but made alive in the spirit.... / 1 Peter 3:18

Alive in the Spirit

My mother was a teacher beyond compare. She taught so many people so many lessons in so many ways, drawing them into her circle of light and love. When she went on to eternal life, I knew her light would live on, especially in my twin daughters who were blessed to spend countless hours learning through play and laughter with my mother. In my mind, I play back the soundtrack of their happy moments. Saying "goodbye" to my mother was difficult. Soon, however, I realized that she wasn't really gone. So much of her spirit lived in me, especially the mothering skills she had taught me. I told my girls that the love, joy, and laughter she shared with us did not die with her frail body. Rather, these traits are forever with us.

I wasn't sure the girls understood until a teacher related my daughter's response to a story about a talented glassblower whose charming heirloom work of art crashed to the floor one Christmas, shattering into hundreds of pieces. Somehow the treasured ornament's spirit and beauty still permeated the room. Rather than lamenting the loss of the ornament, those present were awed by the sense of love and joy that remained. When my daughter heard this, she exclaimed, "That's just like my grandmother. Her body broke but her love and joy are all around me!"

For Meditation
- When the world seems to shatter around me, where do I turn to find love, joy, and hope?
- How can I pass on parenting skills to the next generation?
- How do I choose to reconcile with those I love?

My Thoughts

20

If God is for us, who is against us? He who did not withhold his own Son, but gave him up for all of us, will [God] not with [Christ] also give us everything else? / Romans 8:31b–32

Serving and being served

As the coordinator of a busy program at our church, my responsibilities can be both overwhelming and fulfilling at the same time. One Sunday when we were scheduled to have a commissioning rite to install a new core team to the parish, I was excited and proud to be the one introducing team members in the parish. Needless to say, I had a lot on my mind that morning. My husband and sons were off camping, so I was alone with my ten-month daughter when I arrived in the parking lot. In the process of unloading my van, I absentmindedly locked both my daughter and the keys in the van. Our new pastor wasn't quite sure what to do when I walked crying into the office, embarrassingly reporting that the ceremony would have to be postponed because my daughter was locked in the van. Thankfully, we were in a church parking lot, where several people came to my rescue. In less than a half-hour, the crisis was averted and we walked into church. Our pastor conveniently worked our experience into his homily, which coincidentally dealt with the daily stresses we all face.

For Meditation
- What are some of the sacrifices I make in my life to serve the larger faith community?
- How can I more gracefully approach the many small challenges I face on a regular basis?
- What is my response when it seems as if everyone or everything is working "against" rather than "for" me?

My Thoughts

The precepts of the LORD are right;
  rejoicing the heart;
the commandment of the Lord is clear,
  enlightening the eyes.... / Psalm 19:8

Someone's mother

I needed her ninety years of wit and wisdom after a tedious day at work. "Honey," she said before walking out the door, "if this here light bulb hadn't burnt out, we never would've had this nice chat."

With that, the wrinkled but energetic stranger was gone. Her tried-and-true words, however, remain in my mind. Outliving all but one of her children, the ninety-something former ranch wife had stopped in the needlework store to replace a light bulb for her stitching lamp and casually mentioned something about "back home." I asked her where that was. To her, my simple question was an invitation to sit and chat a while (a while being thirty or forty minutes—the kind of break we rarely take in a work day). To me, her witty tales and knowing eyes were a welcome break after four uninterrupted hours on my feet. She talked about love and child-rearing (her devoted husband had died about thirty years prior), responsibility and hard work. She talked of loneliness and broken hearts, hurt feelings and attempts at reconciliation. I nodded and added my two cents when it seemed appropriate. At one point, she told me, "Girly, you musta' been around."

"Not nearly as much as you," I responded admirably. Since then, I have meditated for hours on her practical wit and wisdom.

For Meditation
- How is hospitality the mark of a Christian?
- What lessons have I learned from strangers? From older people?
- How can I teach my children to respect their elders by my behavior?

My Thoughts

"We know that this is our son, and that he was born blind; but we do not know how it is that now he sees, nor do we know who opened his eyes." / John 9:20–21

Healing pain

The very same day that a dear friend's husband was undergoing brain surgery to remove a cluster of tumors, I was totally distracted by pain—pain for him and his family as well as my own emotional pain. Whether his growth was malignant or benign, it had to be removed. Our church community prayed together in a ten-hour vigil.

As my own tears flowed, I experienced pain over strained relationships in my extended family. I wondered why this pain would come to my mind at this time. It seemed far different than how I felt about a friend facing major surgery. Or was it? For a long time, I had been fighting the need to let go of my anger. I seemed to want to hang on and say, "The tension is not my fault." But, I realized that just as a tumor must be taken out, so too the growth of my anger, resentment, and self-righteousness must be removed. It interfered with my healthy living. I wondered where to look for peace and God's grace. I prayed for strength to forgive those who trespass against me and to freely accept God's love.

For Meditation

- When strained relationships linger on in our extended families, pain intensifies. How can I let go and attain peace of mind?
- What will help me understand that God's time or plan and mine might not always agree?
- How can I make all my suffering positive and life-giving like Jesus did?

My Thoughts

"The Teacher is here and is calling for you." And when she heard it, she got up quickly and went to him." / John 11:28–29

I need you!

My little one was sick. We've all been there as mothers—feeling helpless and concerned over one so precious to us. "Mommy, I need you!" the call came again.

As I went to her bedside, my mind raced with what else I could possibly do to help her. I began the litany, "Do you want a cool washcloth? How about another purple pill? Maybe a story would make you feel better. How about a song? A back rub?"

To everything, her answer was, "No."

Finally, when I quit asking, she gave me her first request, a request I hadn't really heard.

"I just need *you* Mommy."

It was at that point that I understood my presence to her was all she needed. I didn't need to "fix" anything. I just needed to *be* with her. As I complied, she soon drifted off into a peaceful sleep.

How difficult it is for me to just *be still*! My daughter helped me realize that I need to learn to come to my heavenly Father and just *be*—to snuggle my hurting soul in God's arms and find peace, as my daughter did with me.

For Meditation
• When my soul is full of troubles, how can I deal with them in a way that brings at least a tiny sense of peace to my heart?
• How can I schedule time to *be still* daily?
• How does silence bring me more in touch with my true feelings and closer to God?

My Thoughts

24

At the name of Jesus
every knee should bend,
in heaven and on earth and under the earth,
and every tongue should confess
that Jesus Christ is Lord…. / Philippians 2:10–11

Simple prayer

I was a prayer leader for a group at my church. One day my two
sons, ages two and four, were helping me prepare for the
meeting. As I placed the prayer candles out on the table, the
youngest came up to the table, glanced at the candle, and put his
hands together to pray, just as we do at mealtime. He recognized
that the candle was a symbol of Christ's light. I had no idea he
could make the connection. My heart filled with pride to think
that our simple family ritual had so much meaning for our young
son. I took time out from my setting-up duties for an impromptu
prayer with my sons, encouraging our four year old to lead us in
his favorite "Angel of God" prayer. It was never so evident to me
that our angels are lighting the way, safeguarding our actions,
ruling our hearts, and guiding our way. I was proud to know that
I was a prayer leader for my family as well as for our group at
church. Christ was present as the center of my life, the center of
our home.

For Meditation
• How do I bring Christ's presence into our home?
• When is the last time I wrote down my heartfelt thoughts?
  My own personal prayers?
• The next time I bring my hands together in prayer, what will I
  be saying to God?

My Thoughts

Do not be alarmed; you are looking for Jesus of Nazareth, who was crucified. He has been raised; he is not here. / Mark 16:6

Believe

Fax machines were new on the market. We plotted and planned, searched for the best features at the most economical price, and moved into the electronic age. We marveled at the technology, amazed that it took seconds instead of days to receive a document from clear across the country (or across the ocean, for that matter). Soon, we took this incredible device for granted, forgetting the convenience that it added to our lives. All the while, we had no idea that little ears and eyes were taking in our fascination and familiarity with the fax machine.

One day, our youngest was standing at my side as I took a slightly rolled up piece of paper from the machine. "Mommy," he asked, "how do they roll that paper up so teeny tiny that it fits in the telephone wires and comes to our house?"

I smiled at his sincerity, trying to come up with some credible answer for a technology I barely understood. While not technically correct, my explanation seemed to satisfy my son.

"Oh," he mused, "so you just put your paper in the machine and trust it will get where you want it to go."

"Yes," I said, "there are some things you just have to believe."

Christ rose from the dead.

For Meditation
• What are some of the things I have to choose to "take on faith?"
• How is technology a help in my life? How is it a hindrance?
• When do I yearn for deeper explanations of life's mysteries? Where can I turn for clarification, more information, or guidance?

My Thoughts

Now the whole group of those who believed were of one heart and soul, and no one claimed private ownership of any possessions, but everything they owned was held in common. / Acts 4:32

When less is more

Transitional housing was a dreaded exile while awaiting completion of our home. But, once we'd weathered five weeks of "doing without," I started reflecting on a valuable lesson: Although it wasn't easy, we learned we can live with less "stuff" than we expected. Our supportive family and friends sustained us not only with a place to rest our heads and fill our bellies but also with peace in our hearts.

Despite their loving kindness, this was a true adjustment. We decided it was healthy to grieve our loss of privacy and routines. Even the children were confused. I missed common comforts. Advent rituals were very different in a hotel room: A construction paper wreath was more prized than ever before. Our temporary homelessness left us with a better understanding of how people living on the streets must feel and how Mary and Joseph must have felt.

The one place that truly felt like home was our church. Liturgy is nourishing and peaceful. We even stopped there between errands for drinks of water or bathroom breaks more than most people do in a lifetime. What this transitional living arrangement did was refocus our priorities. It even helped us to identify with the Holy Family and their search for a place to rest.

For Meditation
- Change isn't always easy. What are some of the changes I have muddled through? What changes brought growth?
- When I focus on my priorities, what could be rearranged?
- What are some of the simple treasures I cherish?

My Thoughts

My little children, I am writing these things to you so that you may not sin. But if anyone does sin, we have an advocate with the Father, Jesus Christ.... / 1 John 2:1

Stay healthy

My sin is ignoring my body—not to the point of slovenliness or unhealthiness, but to the point where I'm wondering what's in store for me twenty years down the road. To the point where I'll need to buy a size larger next time I hit the sales. I've already hit the scales and I don't like what I see. Still, I resist doing what I know is right and good for the body God gave me.

A decade or so ago, I had an aerobics instructor who exuded confidence and poise. Both her antics and acrobatics made me feel as if I had two left feet. (It's important to note that coordination never has been one of my strong points.) Her cheerful encouragement was exactly what I needed to rid myself of some excess post-childbirth flab. I never grew to enjoy sweating off the pounds, but I did come to tolerate the routines and the benefits.

Then, gradually, my schedule got cluttered. Exercise was the first activity to be moved to the back burner. Way back! It has been a year since I walked regularly and longer since I touched a weight. I tell myself I want to change but keep sabotaging my own efforts. I need to turn to someone more powerful for help. Are you listening, Lord?

For Meditation
• What do I do to take care of my body, a temple of the Holy Spirit?
• How do I nurture my family's health, nutrition, and need for exercise?
• How can I enhance my emotional well-being?

My Thoughts

"I am the good shepherd. The good shepherd lays down his life for the sheep." / John 10:11

Flexibility or frustration?

As a new mother, my greatest challenge was flexibility. Making a plan, making a list, focusing—these had been the secret of my success throughout school and in my career. I could hardly believe that an infant—so small, so helpless, so dependent, so immovable—could be the disruption of all my plans for accomplishing the day's work. Eventually, I learned to let go. My choices were flexibility or frustration. So what if getting showered and dressed by 4 P.M. was my only personal accomplishment in a day? People, especially my precious children, were more important than things.

Now in midlife, I look back, amazed, because I now find myself so flexible that I often have trouble focusing on anyone or anything before I'm off in another direction. My DayTimer is completely abandoned. Will I recapture the abilities of my youth? Will I ever choose to be that organized again?

For Meditation
- How can flexibility help get me through the difficult days?
- When I recall the sage words from Ecclesiastes, "To every season there is a purpose...," how can I better accept the phases and changes in my life?
- What happens when I focus on my God-given strengths and virtues instead of delving into my past?

My Thoughts

"You kept me safe on my mother's breast." / Psalm 22:9

Holy darkness

There's something about those 2 A.M. feedings that a mother
will never forget. In Michigan the winter nights can be very cold,
dark, and still. My son was a winter baby. I would awaken to his
robust cries. Groggy with sleep, I would pad across the hall and
recline in the rocking chair to feed him. When I held him next
to my breast, his warmth and the flowing milk brought on a
certain calm and contentment. One night while rocking,
I exclaimed aloud to the darkness, "I wonder who else is up at
this awful hour besides me?"

To my surprise, through the darkness came a reassuring reply,
"There are people across the ocean praying. Why not join them?"

After this spiritual awakening, the 2 A.M. feedings—still
disruptive to my sleep—acquired a new meaning. Unknowingly,
I had been introduced to the prayer of silence. The prayer of
silence is sometimes called the prayer of the heart, the prayer of
simplicity, Christian meditation, and/or centering prayer. It is a
silent prayer in which we open up our whole being to the
ultimate mystery of life, beyond words, images, thoughts, and
feelings. It is a beautiful way of being with God.

I know people were praying across the ocean because years
later my son and his wife would adopt a baby from Korea.

For Meditation
• How comfortable am I with silence?
• What do I hear in the silence?
• How can I help my children to appreciate moments of silence?

My Thoughts

30

Beloved, let us love one another, because love is from God; everyone who loves is born of God and knows God. Whoever does not love does not know God, for God is love. / 1 John 4:7–8

Beauty

We were blessed with many foster children. The first had a ready smile and sparkling brown eyes. We loved her, cared for her, and proudly passed her to her new, adoring parents, knowing that she would be treasured. Next came a strong, comely little fellow who charmed everyone he met. What a happy occasion it was to hand him to his new parents. A girl followed, then a boy and more. Each baby was absorbed into the loving arms of adoptive parents.

Then came a child who cried and fussed most of her waking moments. She was not lovely. She ate poorly and refused to be soothed. She offered nothing in return for the many hours of patience and nurturing she received. It took determination to love this child. The time came to present her to her new family. She cried in the car. She fussed through her feeding. She messed her new clothes. With trepidation we passed her to the waiting arms of her new parents. The mother pulled back the blanket from her face, peered into the tear-streaked face of the unhappy baby and said quietly, "Isn't she the most beautiful child you have ever seen?"

She stroked the baby's cheek. The child quieted.

For Meditation
• When have I loved even when it seemed impossible?
• How have I opened my home, my arms, and my heart to those in need?
• Who loves me during my most unlovable moments?

My Thoughts

"Go into all the world and proclaim the good news to the whole creation. The one who believes and is baptized will be saved…."
Mark 16:15–16

Wise ones

I've always associated wisdom with the experience that comes through living a long life. So, I was somewhat surprised when my own children had moments of amazing wisdom. I mean, not everyone can figure out how to divide two Popsicles five ways. (Melt them and pour the remains into five small cups). How about their recipe for mending hurt feelings? (Gathering a bouquet of fragrant weeds that turned out to be terrible allergens.) Then there was the rescue effort when our children were determined to save the snails from the deadly bait we scattered about the yard. (They forgot to feed and water them once in captivity and before long, the snails had succumbed to their fate only to receive the requisite funeral and time of mourning.)

Certainly, age does bring on a special kind of wisdom. But, right now, I'm content to revel in the innocent and simple wisdom my children deliver.

For Meditation
- Of the lessons children have taught me, what are the most valuable?
- Do I proclaim the Good News to all creation? How?
- Am I aging gracefully, taking time to reflect on my own experiences?

My Thoughts

"And now I am no longer in the world, but they are in the world, and I am coming to you. Holy Father, protect them in your name that you have given me, so that they may be one, as we are one." / John 17:11

Field trips in my mind

It was the morning of what likely would be the last field trip for mother and son. These periodic adventures seem to end when high school starts—either that or the kids are too embarrassed to have mom and dad along as chaperones. The end of eighth grade was approaching for my youngest and we were preparing a sack lunch for our outing to a science museum. His only concern was making certain there were enough chips and cookies in the sack to satisfy the appetite of a fourteen year old. My thoughts were of a less practical bent, struggling to recall those first field trips some fifteen years ago when our oldest was in preschool.
At times like this I wish I had been a journal keeper. What a joy it would be to return to those adventures to the zoo and the ice cream factory and the opera (well, the latter might not fall into the joyful category). Now, I smile remembering our sweaty backs and damp hair as we rode unairconditioned school buses, the poor sound systems in some auditoriums and the antics of rowdy students. From here on out, the field trips I take will be in my mind. Meanwhile, I pray that my children and I will continue to love the adventures of new ideas and new places.

For Meditation
• How do I make transitions in my life?
• Jesus had confidence that his Father would care for all of creation. Why am I sometimes so lacking in confidence?
• What is my response to new ideas and new places?

My Thoughts

Now there are varieties of gifts, but the same Spirit; and there are
varieties of services, but the same Lord; and there are varieties of
activities, but it is the same God who activates all of them in everyone.
To each is given the manifestation of the Spirit for the common good.
1 Corinthians 12:4–7

Medicine and mini-miracles

The peace and quiet of a summer evening were interrupted when
our toddlers collided and the oldest needed stitches. Off we went
to the emergency room, with mom (also being very pregnant)
more nervous than anyone else in the car. While this adventure
might be routine to some, it was new to our family. As the
doctors prepped our son for stitches, he asked him which parent
he wanted to stay with him through the procedure. Although I
was relieved when he chose his father, waiting outside the door
still was not easy. I heard his cries as the anesthetic was injected.
When I fell to my knees in prayer, passers-by assumed something
was wrong and that I needed help. When I told them I was
praying the rosary, they smiled but clearly were surprised by or
didn't understand my response. I kept praying, and I believe his
spirit calmed as a result. I was reminded of the power of prayer
and the miracles of modern medicine. We are all united in one
Spirit to soothe pain in each other.

For Meditation
- When I take inventory of my gifts, do I ever get down on my
  knees to thank God for them?
- What prayer styles work best to express my relationship with
  God? Am I comfortable trying new forms of prayer?
- Medicine brings countless miracles our way. How can I show
  my appreciation for those in the healing professions?

My Thoughts

For all who are led by the Spirit of God are children of God. For you did not receive a spirit of slavery to fall back into fear, but you have received a spirit of adoption. When we cry, "Abba! Father!" it is that very Spirit bearing witness with our spirit that we are children of God.... / Romans 8:14–16

Dad

My dad taught me countless lessons, the last being one of the most poignant: Suffering, he showed all of us, truly can be a blessing. Always a fighter, dad felt he was a victor whether he won his battle with cancer or not. "If I'm cured, I continue this life on earth. If I'm not," he said with the utmost conviction, "I'll be in heaven with God."

I'm certain dad is in heaven now, marveling that his children, God's children, still revel in the spiritual legacy he left us. First, his example showed us that placing *all* of our trust in God is essential. He modeled the virtues of hard work and the importance of family life. He believed in miracles. Even before his illness, dad lived as if every single day was a gift. He encouraged our spiritual development and challenged us to live and pass on Gospel truths.

In the end, dad lovingly shared with us the fact that death is a process, not an event. Yes, it is a painful process but a tremendous growth experience for all members of the Body of Christ.

For Meditation
- As a child of God, what are my responsibilities to my brothers and sisters in Christ?
- How can I be supportive when someone I love is faced with the knowledge that death is near?
- Am I open to seeking comfort from others in times of personal grief?

My Thoughts

...and all the people answered with one voice, and said, "All the words that the LORD has spoken we will do. / Exodus 24:3

The gift of grace

With nine children, my mother had little time for uninterrupted prayer. She taught each of us that grace-filled moments can be found in ordinary tasks, if we simply offered them up to God. "By doing this," she said, "you'll see the work of God's hands in yours. You'll see God's love in all you do. Then, even the most menial of jobs will become a meaningful and spiritual experience shared with God."

My mother's passing on of this incredible spiritual insight was a true gift of grace for me. Her simple and genuinely loving ways remain guidelines for my own actions. Mundane tasks may never be glamorous, yet they take on so much more meaning for me because of the example set by my own mother.

For Meditation
- How can I be more aware and appreciative of the grace-filled moments that make up my day?
- What are my feelings when I recognize that my hands are an extension of God's hands?
- When am I challenged by others who don't appreciate or value menial, mundane tasks?

My Thoughts

*"Do not fear, only believe…Why do you make a commotion and
weep? The child is not dead but sleeping."* And they laughed at him.
Mark 5:36,39–40

A prayer for a friend

A dear friend's daughter had passed away at the tender age of
eight after battling a rare and terminal genetic disease. Almost a
year had passed and I was settling my boys (six and eight) down
for bed. As is our practice, we recite three prayers followed by
what I refer to as the "Three P's"—Praise, what we're thankful
for; Pardon, what we're sorry for; and Petition, where we need to
seek God's help for ourselves or another.

The youngest announced that he wanted to pray for the friend
who died. "Oh no," I thought to myself, "he has forgotten that
she died. He's going to pray for her healing. We're going to have
to go through this all over again."

But, before my thoughts went into words, he continued,
"Because she's in heaven now and she's very happy because she
doesn't need her wheelchair anymore and she can swallow and
run around and play and everything!"

Tears filled my eyes as I realized that not only did he
understand the permanence of death but he also understood the
greater mystery of heaven.

Lord, I prayed. Give me a childlike faith!

For Meditation
• When is my faith like that of a child?
• How have I prepared myself and my family for life eternal?
• When do my tears of joy mingle with tears of grief?

My Thoughts

And when he spoke to me, a spirit entered into me and set me on my feet; and I heard him speaking to me. He said to me, Mortal, I am sending you to the people of Israel…. I am sending you to them, and you shall say to them, "Thus says the Lord GOD." / Ezekiel 2:2–4

Delightful days

Finally, well into my second decade of motherhood, I'm learning to delight in the simple things. Just delight. Not worry. Not analyze. Not fret. Not look forward. Not plan. Not glance back. I am satisfied with what is, with who I am.

Delightful days aren't made; they just happen. A delightful day can be one that begins with rain on the window sill, a perfect day for curling up under an afghan on the couch. It can be one that's so frantic we barely remember our hello and goodbye hugs. A delightful day can be one filled with challenges or one devoid of pressure. It can take me into the city or leave me in my cozy suburban home. Delight, I've learned, comes from within and radiates out to encourage and nurture delight in others. Precious memories can make any day delightful because they transport us to comfortable places in our hearts.

For Meditation
• What has taught me to wait patiently for the Lord?
• How can I make my home the place where, as author Sarah Josepha Hale said more than 130 years ago, we spend our "best and happiest hours?"
• In what do I most delight?

My Thoughts

Then Amos answered Amaziah, "I am no prophet, nor a prophet's son; but I am a herdsman, and a dresser of sycamore trees, and the LORD took me from following the flock, and the LORD said to me, 'Go, prophesy to my people Israel.'" / Amos 7:14–15

Those colicky babies

I received the good news that I was pregnant. It was the news for which I had been waiting, so I was ready. I ate healthy meals. Gained the right weight. Read the appropriate books. Listened to classical music. It turned out to be a wonderful pregnancy and flawless delivery. I brought a healthy baby home. Everything was perfect.

Fifteen days later the person I was holding in my hands was an inconsolable baby, one the experts call a "colicky baby." I was not ready for this! Now, four-and-a-half years later, I look back and reflect on the experience along with other women who are blessed—yes, I said blessed—with colicky babies. In our helplessness and despair, we watch our babies endure hour after of hour of apparent pain and inconsolable crying. We persevere with them day and night. We lift our hearts to the Lord. We pray for our babies. We love them and hold them tight. Then, we look at the essence of our souls and ask God to console us. We grow spiritually and abundantly in all aspects of our lives. Thank you, God, for holding us in your arms.

For Meditation
- Who are the "colicky babies" I hold in my arms?
- What blessings come to me in disguise, strengthening me beyond my limits?
- What are some of the special tasks with which God has asked me to persevere day and night?

My Thoughts

So he came and proclaimed peace to you who were far off and peace to those who were near.... / Ephesians 2:17

I am a mom

My weary knees carry me upstairs for the twelfth, thirteenth,
    even eighteenth time today.
I am a mom.
My hands reach, robot like, into the hamper,
    separating dark from light.
I am a mom.
My nail snags on the yarn of a torn navy sock.
I am a mom.
My head swims full of "to-dos" for tomorrow is only Tuesday.
I am a mom.
My neighbor can barely move from her hospital bed.
She is a mom.
We share one spirit.
It is our God.
God loves moms.

For Meditation
• Why is it so difficult for me to find peace at certain times
  in my life?
• What are a few proclamations I can make in favor of peace?
• How can I encourage my children to seek out a peaceful
  lifestyle?

My Thoughts

*Then Jesus took the loaves, and when he had given thanks, he
distributed them to those who were seated; so also the fish, as much
as they wanted. When they were satisfied, he told his disciples,
"Gather up the fragments left over, so that nothing may be lost."*
John 6:11–12

Home picnic

The seemingly longer-than-usual winter in Minnesota found my
three children (ten, eight, and four) cooped up inside once again
with our two black Labradors. We all roamed the house
aimlessly, not able to go outside because of the thawing mess.
There we were: Three kids and a mom who felt as if she was
losing her sanity.

Never at a loss for creativity, the children grabbed a blanket,
hauled out a stack of encyclopedias and made a tent. Our family
room was a disaster. Upstairs, I searched the cupboards for yet
another un-gourmet dinner. What to make? The same old call in
the wilderness that every mother makes through the years.

Suddenly an idea came to me: What about a picnic in the
living room? I spread the red and white checkered tablecloth and
put the portable boom box in the center, playing summer tunes.
I sat out the hot dogs, chips, pickles, soda, and cookies. And, yes,
as I called the kids up from downstairs, I was dancing.
They joined in. Daddy's "What's this" needed no answer when
he walked in the door. He joined right in.

Looking back, I wonder why I hadn't used creativity more
often as a solution rather than frustration or discipline.
Who needs clean carpets when we can have winter picnics?

For Meditation
• How can I be more creative?
• What nourishes my creative spirit?
• How do children and grandchildren inspire me?

My Thoughts

For we did not follow cleverly devised myths when we made known to you the power and coming of our Lord Jesus Christ, but we had been eyewitnesses of his majesty. For he received honor and glory from God the Father when that voice was conveyed to him by the Majestic Glory, saying, "This is my Son, my Beloved, with whom I am well pleased." We ourselves heard this voice come from heaven, while we were with him on the holy mountain. / 2 Peter 1:16–18

Uncertainty

Because I married young and was so young when I had my first child, I was quite insecure about my mothering skills. I listened yet was bombarded with advice about infants and schedules and child-rearing and family life. I had a difficult time making decisions about my children when the advice I was hearing conflicted with my own ideas. Lack of self-confidence caused me to be uncertain whether my choices were "right" or "wrong."

It was a spiritual growth group that helped me see motherhood as my ministry. I saw my children as a precious gift from God. And, if I trusted the giver of this gift, I could have faith in my decisions—whether they be right or wrong. Suddenly, my choices were affirmed.

Now when people give me advice about motherhood, I listen with a new confidence that my own thoughts and choices are valid and often the "right" ones.

For Meditation
• How do I react when my friends or relatives are judgmental?
• Who is the "cheerleader" that affirms my choices and actions?
• When I listen, is it with understanding and concern rather than judgment?

My Thoughts

"Do not complain among yourselves." / John 6:43

Gather my scattered thoughts, O Lord

"Sensory overload" is a near-perfect way to describe how I felt some days. Requests funnel in from every direction: Mom, where are my ballet shoes? Mom can I use the computer? Ma'am, you're overdue for an oil change. Can you be at the parent meeting Monday? Did you know you have seventeen overdue library books? You will be at the staff meeting, won't you? How about lunch next Thursday? The list seems endless.

I love my life! I love the many roles I have in it and even the mundane yet satisfying challenges it presents. When (and if) I have time to sit down at the end of every day to collect my thoughts for the next day, I have a big request for God. I ask God to accompany me on the journey and to impart a bit of the Holy Spirit's wisdom in this oft-confused mind.

For Meditation
- What impact does complaining have within my household? How can or do we avoid complaining?
- When everyone wants a piece of me, what portion of myself do I reserve just for myself?
- Those who wrote the Scriptures seemed to have the time, insight, and energy to accomplish great things. How could I use writing to jot down memorable words?

My Thoughts

Be careful then how you live, not as unwise people but as wise,
making the most of the time , because the days are evil. So do not
be foolish, but understand what the will of the Lord is.
Ephesians 5:15–17

Absent

I don't know when it dawned on me that I was absent from my
household. Physically, I was present. I drove to Scouts. I listened
to heartbreaks. I wiped a few tears. I counseled. I cooked and
cleaned. I tried to keep everyone healthy. I also worked and read
and kept a nearly weed-free garden. I volunteered at church and
at school and at the art center. But, despite all of the running
around and playing around I did, my heart didn't feel the fruits of
my efforts.

Lord, I thought I was making the most of the time you gave
me. I was filling it with activities and "busyness," but I wasn't
being careful how I lived. Some of my choices were unwise just
because they took me away from you and from myself. Thank
you for helping me get back on track. Thank you for helping me
understand that I am valuable as a person, that my value doesn't
rest in how much I do but in how much I love.

For Meditation
• What are my family's favorite pastimes? How do we make the
most of our time together?
• How can I become more in tune to the will of the Lord?
Do I have a spiritual mentor?
• How do (did) I pass on to my children the wisdom that helps
them develop their own sense of spirituality?

My Thoughts

"As for me and my household, we will serve the LORD." / Joshua 24:15

She serves

Of all the people I've known, there is one whose boundless energy serves the Lord every waking moment. Her professional career encompasses both nursing care and church ministry. Believing that all of life is sacred, she takes her convictions from the board room to homeless dining rooms. She gets her hands dirty and does not shy away from controversy. Her family watches, in loving support, knowing she'll be there at dance recitals and other performances. She always worships with her family, thanking God for the energy and wisdom to help carry out her convictions. Her wry sense of humor eases even the toughest of tensions, reminding those around her that no problem is so big it can't be solved. She knows when to tread lightly, when to exert her influence. She is honest and open, caring and loving. She stands as an icon of service, never seeking praise or recognition. She eschews praise, asking only that those around her do what they can to build up the Body of Christ. Our world is a better place because of women like this.

For Meditation
• What rituals are important to me in our family's efforts to serve the Lord?
• For some, nurturing comes naturally. For others, it requires conscious effort. How can I better nurture myself and those I love?
• When do I go beyond my comfort zone to serve the Lord by serving others?

My Thoughts

Every generous act of giving, with every perfect gift, is from above,
coming down from the Father of lights, with whom there is no
variation or shadow due to change…be doers of the word, and not
merely hearers who deceive themselves…. / James 1:17,22

What's inside

Mom kept her buttons in a colorful cigar box. Mine are in a
squatty old marshmallow jar with a rusted tin lid. Growing up,
I remember needing to replace missing shirt buttons or those
all-essential waistband fasteners. Whatever I needed was always
somewhere in that cigar box. At times it contained glorious and
colorful buttons, rescued from a no-longer-needed dress. Other
times, the contents included mainly utilitarian white buttons,
snaps, and hooks. At times, my button jar contains a vast supply
of fasteners. Other times—like right after a craft project—it's
nearly empty. These purely utilitarian containers have some
amazing parallels to life.

It doesn't matter what the container is like on the
outside—some are large, others small. Some are stylish, others
ragged and worn. What matters is what's inside. We need to do
whatever we can to keep the inside as well stocked as possible,
ready for any eventuality.

For Meditation
• What are some of the trinkets and treasures I cherish? Where
do I store them?
• When I deceive myself, how do I feel? When others deceive
me, how do I feel?
• How do I refresh and renew my spirit following good deeds that
zap my energy?

My Thoughts

46

Say to those who are of a fearful heart,
  "Be strong, do not fear!
Here is your God.
  He will come with vengeance,
with terrible recompense.
  He will come and save you." / Isaiah 35:4

Nieces are nice

My six-year-old niece was playing outside one fall afternoon
and found a sick blue jay barely alive lying by the driveway.
She quickly summoned her dad, asking him if she could try to
save the bird. They found the requisite shoebox, a soft towel
(mom was gone shopping, so no doubt it was one of her best),
and a dish for some water. Then they lovingly placed the bird in
the box and brought the box into the utility room.

"Keep it in the back of your mind," Dad cautioned, "that the
bird might not make it. The bird could die during the night."

My niece thought for a moment and said, "If it makes it
through the night, can I bring it to the front of my mind?"

The bird lived and the next morning, to everyone's delight,
was taken outside to be set free.

For Meditation
• How does the promise of eternal salvation bring me hope?
• What thoughts do I keep in the back of my mind out of fear?
• When injury, illness, or disaster cause me to be fearful, how
  and where do I find consolation? How have I faced my fear?

My Thoughts

The Lord GOD has opened my ear.... / Isaiah 50:5

"It's singing for me!"

One spring morning, I woke up tired, grouchy, and far from God. My oldest son, then three, was perched on his booster seat, ready for breakfast. My second son, then one, was in his highchair. Our newest addition, in the womb, was causing a wave of nausea to sweep over me. I began clamoring around the kitchen, trying to sort through the tasks that lay before me, when my oldest child startled me with a large and dramatic, "Shhh!"

I looked over at him and he put his finger to his lips saying, "Listen! There's a bird outside this window singing for me!"

Well, my first reaction was to think that I had read one too many articles on how to boost my child's self-esteem while pregnant. But, as I looked at the joy on his face, and as I listened to the bird's sweet song, I believed him. He was right! That bird had been sent to sing for him and the miracle was that he heard it and shared his joyful discovery with a grouchy mom. It made me wonder how many "birds" God sends to me that I'm too busy or too loud to hear. When I do hear, how often does my fear of others' opinions keep me from sharing the "song?"

For Meditation
• How do I celebrate nature and its glorious seasons?
• What portion of every day do I spend listening for the birds and watching flowers bloom?
• What fuels my heart? What do I need to strengthen my soul?

My Thoughts

Then he took a little child and put it among them; and taking it in his arms, he said to them, "Whoever welcomes one such child in my name welcomes me, and whoever welcomes me welcomes not me but the one who sent me." / Mark 9:35–37

Dual races

In the spring of 1993, I was in a race to complete my master's degree before the birth of our first child. Both were "due" on the same day. Eight months pregnant, I sat in an auditorium with fifty other students writing the six-hour comprehensive exams required prior to graduation. As my right hand methodically recorded my essay, my left hand soothingly followed the path of my son's lumpy foot across my rounded belly.

When I think back to that experience, it seems symbolic of what motherhood has given me. Amidst the business of taking my exams, my child—through his most intimate connection with me—provided comfort and amusement just by the wonder of his presence. As the mother of two young sons, I wonder if Jesus was consoled and even humored by the little children he met. My sons give love without fear of being hurt. They are true to their little personalities. They freely acknowledge the pain they cause each other. The purity of their love eases my adult misgivings and enlivens me to accept the challenges I believe God has set out for me—as a woman, as a mother, and, most importantly, as a child of God.

For Meditation
- What "races" do I run in my life that could be slowed down or toned down to a less frantic pace?
- In what ways do we welcome Christ into our family life?
- How does my understanding of a child-like nature help me to put life in perspective?

My Thoughts

Let the words of my mouth and the meditation of my heart
  be acceptable to you,
  O LORD, my rock and my redeemer. / Psalm 19:14

Voices from afar

We were clear across the country, in a new town, a new home,
and a new parish. Wanting to get involved right away, I agreed
to help facilitate a MOMS group. The only person I had ever
even met there was the other facilitator. En route to that first
gathering, I was getting pretty nervous. Out of nowhere, I heard
a gentle voice from back home urging me, "Get over it." In my
mind, she jokingly chided me—as she had done so many times in
the past—not to get over-excited, as was my tendency.
This voice from afar worked like magic. I felt a calm come over
me recalling the first time I ever met this friend. She was the
facilitator of my MOMS group. She grew to become a true friend.
As I drove on, I realized it was a week short of the anniversary of
her unexpected death at age thirty-seven. Using her strength as
my inspiration, I knew I would do just fine in my role as
facilitator.

For Meditation
• When do my words, actions, and meditations most reflect the
  harmony and balance I seek in life?
• Even during dreary and unpleasant times, God, my rock and
  redeemer, is present. How do I call upon God's strength?
  How do I gain strength from others?
• What friends are there to support me when I have personal
  doubts and misgivings?

My Thoughts

Then the LORD God said, "It is not good that the man should be alone; I will make him a helper as his partner." / Genesis 2:18

Appreciation

I thought I knew so much about relationships when I got married: Love would conquer all. Love would span the oceans and vast expanses of land between us. Love would provide the freshly painted cottage with a white picket fence. Love would sustain us, even on the tightest of budgets. Love would be all we would need to live in eternal bliss.

Five years into marriage, the love was strong but an apartment was home. Ten years of wedded bliss (or near-bliss) and the love was there, but we hadn't found the picket fence. Fifteen years and two children later, the love was gaining a bit of wisdom, realizing that it took hard work to put food on the table. Twenty years later, the love is still there, continually growing wiser and finally outgrowing some of the naive expectations. The love we share today has taken on a more practical and realistic tone, finding time for romance amidst wild schedules and myriad commitments. As love looks to retirement, who knows? That white picket fence just might be waiting for us on a cliff above the sea.

For Meditation
• How have my ideas of commitment changed over the years? Where has love taken my commitments?
• Do I freely share my dreams with my husband? My best friend? My children? My parents?
• What is required to sustain relationships over long periods of time?

My Thoughts

Therefore I prayed, and understanding was given me;
I called on God, and the spirit of wisdom came to me. / Wisdom 7:7

Recovering

I am a recovering yeller. My children had grown accustomed to my vocal outbursts over the years. One of my biggest challenges was when my children would fight. When a friend suggested that I consider asking my squabbling children to join me in prayer, I had nothing to lose.

The next time a skirmish erupted, I asked them to join me in prayer. They looked more than a bit bewildered by my request but knelt down in compliance. I don't remember the words of our prayer, but I do know it had an impact on our method of conflict resolution.

A week or so later, I heard my daughter scream. When I ran to the rescue, I found my son holding her in a head lock. As soon as he saw me, he released his hold, helped her up and asked, "Is it time to pray, Mom?"

For Meditation
- What are some of the creative solutions we use to resolve conflict at home?
- How are conflicts on the job resolved?
- What sense of wisdom do I get when I call on the Holy Spirit?

My Thoughts

"Whoever wishes to be first among you must be slave of all. For the Son of Man came not to be served but to serve, and to give his life a ransom for many." / Mark 10:44–45

Community service: More than a project

"How can I get this out of the way in a hurry?" my daughter pleaded when scheduling required community service time for school.

"Thirty hours is thirty hours," I responded in true motherly fashion, "but a good attitude just might help the time pass a little faster."

Several weeks passed and I hadn't heard of any progress. Then one day she announced she was going to a local elder-care facility to deliver some cards. I was surprised when her quick trip turned into a five-hour visit.

At dinner that evening, all she wanted to do was recount her experience visiting with old folks who hadn't had visitors in weeks. "Mom, you can't imagine the smiles on their faces. Some of them were out of it, but they were still happy to see us. I don't think I ever saw someone so happy just to see me."

And my daughter thought she was the one providing the "service."

For Meditation
- What would happen in my community if everyone just gave an hour of community service each week? If I had a couple extra hours of time, where would I donate it?
- How can I encourage my children to be more involved in the lives of those who could use their help?
- What chores could we do to better serve one another in our home?

My Thoughts

…those with children and those in labor, together…
they shall come,
  and with consolations, I will lead them back,
I will let them walk by brooks of water,
  in a straight path in which they shall not stumble….
Jeremiah 31:8–9

Journey with God

My husband and I are in the process of opening a Crisis
Pregnancy Center. Along the journey with God, we have faced
many obstacles and challenges. At a retreat focusing on the
Beatitudes, I was able to talk about our struggles in terms of
"Blessed are those who are persecuted for the sake of
righteousness, for theirs is the kingdom of heaven."

The choice of opening the center has strained some of my
friendships. We've even had friends think we're planning an
abortion clinic bombing—which couldn't be further from the truth.

At the end of the retreat, a woman sought me out. Wearing
her heart on her shirt sleeve, she apologized so sincerely,
thinking she had been one of those who had caused us pain.
As I struggled to keep my jaw from hitting the ground, I assured her
I was not referring to her. In fact, she had never entered my mind.

The friend sitting next to me said, "Wow, you handled that
with a lot of grace."

It wasn't until later that I wondered who handled the
situation with grace: Was it me or the woman who felt
compelled to seek me out?

For Meditation
• When I feel persecuted, how do I respond?
• How can I handle more situations with grace and courage?
• When have I taken a stand and followed it through?

My Thoughts

The first of all commandments:
*You shall love the Lord your God with all your heart, and with all
your soul, and with all your might. Keep these words that I am
commanding you today in your heart. Recite them to your children
and talk about them when you are at home and when you are away,
when you lie down and when you rise.* / Deuteronomy 6:5–7

The second:
To love one's neighbor as oneself… / Mark 12:33

On exhibit

An ornate beaded box created more than three centuries ago
was on display in colonial Williamsburg, Virginia. Of all the
beautiful handwork in the exhibit, this one called to me—not
because of its colors or design (there were far more beautiful
items on display). The sentiment expressed is what spoke to me.
Inscribed across the top edge were the words, "In God set all thy
heart's joy and delight forever more." What a lesson for life!
I repeated that phrase to myself over and over, wondering who
had taken the time to sew on each tiny glass bead that formed
each letter. Did she believe those words? Did she struggle as we
do today? Was her heart full of joy and delight? Did she have any
idea that her treasure would somehow survive for hundreds of
years to be admired by visitors to an historical gallery? Tiny
inspirations are all around us waiting to be discovered!

For Meditation
• What reminds me how much God loves me?
• What do I treasure about my ancestors?
• What have I done lately to show that I love my neighbors?

My Thoughts

A poor widow came and put in two small copper coins, which are worth a penny…. [S]he out of her poverty has put in everything she had, all she had to live on." / Mark 12:42,44

He chose to give

We were returning home from vacation when we stopped at a nondescript road-side diner somewhere in the middle of the desert. En route from the restaurant back to the car, each of us passed a homeless man drinking from an outside spigot. My heart went out to him, yet I curbed my desire to offer him a few dollars.
The somber tone when we got back in the car belied the fun we had experienced during the past week. About twenty minutes down the road, my husband and I turned to each other and started speaking at the same time. Each of us expressed our disappointment at not having offered the man some money, even though he had made no requests. We pledged never to let that happen again.

Not ten minutes after returning home, our son came to visit, asking about our trip. We told him about the beach and sights but didn't mention the man by the restaurant. When we asked what our son had been doing, he said, "I made a homeless man cry today." With a quick and overly sensitive, "Why," both my husband and I gave each other one of those curious glances.

"I gave him some money," he responded.

With those five words, our decisions and our years of parenting were reaffirmed. I prayed for God's blessings on my son and on all God's children.

For Meditation
- What are some of the unexpected discoveries I've made in the process of living out my faith?
- What are the most meaningful achievements of my life?
- What actions show my faith?

My Thoughts

"Many of those who sleep in the dust of the earth shall awake, some to everlasting life, and some to shame and everlasting contempt. Those who are wise shall shine like the brightness of the sky, and those who lead many to righteousness, like the stars forever and ever."
Daniel 12:2–3

Hot sauce wisdom

One evening when we were enjoying a bowl of chili, I noticed my four year old staring intently at a bottle of hot sauce containing a picture of "the devil." The creature's red countenance, horns, flaring nostrils, and pitchfork propelled my son into deep thought. He soon asked where the devil lived. I tried my best to explain the concept of hell as a place of discomfort, but that if we worked hard throughout our lives and were kind to others we wouldn't have to worry about that eventuality. He then asked how we actually get into heaven. I told him I wasn't certain of the logistics, but that when it was time, God would let us know.

As he sat there contemplating, I began to wonder about my explanation. Suddenly he broke the silence, "I think that when it's time to go to heaven, we change energy."

Hmm, I thought. That's probably a logical, understandable explanation of going to heaven. I also realized that not only did God send my children to me so that I may "train them in the way they should go" but also so I can "become as little children." Obviously, my children know God. They have proven to be my greatest teachers.

For Meditation
• What are my concepts of heaven and hell?
• How can the messages I impart to my children live on "like the stars forever and ever"?
• Whom do I need to thank for helping me understand the wonders of the universe?

My Thoughts

"I am the Alpha and the Omega," says the Lord God, who is and who was and who is to come, the Almighty. / Revelation 1:8

All circuits busy

I don't know how many times I've picked up the phone and dialed a call only to be disappointed by the message, "We are sorry. All circuits are now busy."

Although that response is aggravating, there are plenty of times when I've wanted to give that response to someone who needed a piece of me.

Fortunately for us, God's circuits never are too busy to respond to our pleas. Perhaps that's what's so awesome about our God. God is all things to all persons throughout all time.

Some years ago, my son asked, "Mom, how big is God?"

Never having contemplated that question, I had to think fast.

"Bigger than my thighs," I joked.

"Come on, Mom," he demanded, "really."

"As big as the sky?" I asked.

"Bigger," he told me.

"As big as the universe?"

"Bigger," he repeated.

"All of infinity tied in a bow multiplied by a trillion?" I ventured.

"Bigger," he insisted.

"Well then, if you know so much, why did you bother asking me?"

"Because, Mom, you always tell us we can ask you anything."

I'm thankful my circuits weren't too busy to play my son's game.

For Meditation
• How do I feel when I ponder the Lord's awesome power?
• What do I need to do so my circuits aren't too busy for others?
• Who are the friends with whom I feel a close connection?

My Thoughts

APPENDIX: MOMSharing —
Using MOMStories in Group Settings

Background: MOMStories and MOMS

For those who have been part of the Ministry of Mothers Sharing (MOMS), it's no secret that the ministry's success is largely attributable to you and your willingness to share your spirit-filled stories as mothers. Whether we're dealing with the everyday stresses that leave us feeling frazzled or the unexpected blessings that fill our lives with delight, we exist to support and affirm one another in the many roles that make up our lives.

We are what make MOMS work. Although the history of MOMS goes back more than decade, the energy that fuels it is as old as time itself. God gave us the wonderful gift of life in our vocation of motherhood. It is through God's grace that we continue to become more aware of the sacredness of our call to motherhood and to the challenges of personal growth. It is these challenges that prompted Sister Paula Hagen, then a coordinator of family ministry, to work with mothers in the parish to develop a ministry designed to provide support, companionship, and a spiritual boost for women who share one role in common: motherhood. Sister Paula taught mothers to create a safe, sacred, and welcoming environment in which they could nourish their souls and share their stories. The ministry has welcomed many mothers back to their place of worship. It has opened the doors to many other ministries.

As this parish-based ministry expanded, requests for materials and support started pouring in from neighboring churches and, soon, from across the country. That's when Sister Paula and I joined our creative talents to write MOMS: A Personal Journal, summarizing key elements of journal writing, sharing stories, and prayer rituals. From there, Patricia Hoyt helped structure the ministry with materials designed for MOMS facilitators and staff developers. Today, the impact of the ministry is seen everywhere from Alaska to Florida, thanks to the dedication of women of all ages across the nation. With the addition of a video (MOMS: What Is It?), leaders are able to provide interested groups with rapid access to an introduction to the spirit-filled ministry. The success of the ministry and the video brought about an increased demand for MOMS retreats, especially on the topics of "Blessings of Motherhood" and "Moms As Storytellers." Mornings and evenings of prayer and reflection also help moms see the Holy Spirit working in their lives.

MOMStories is an opportunity for us to continue sharing the enthusiasm we experience in our MOMS groups, retreats, and celebrations. For those who want to use MOMStories for ongoing groups, the ministry's founder, Sister Paula Hagen, has developed a format for ongoing groups, which appears on the next page. Included after the suggested format is a page of "Group Rules for Ongoing Groups," first published in the 1995 book MOMS: Developing a Ministry. Both pages may be photocopied and distributed among group leaders (but please see limitation on the copyright page of this book.)

Suggested Format for Using MOMStories to Continue the Journey

For those who have participated in the eight-week MOMS program, the three-member Facilitator Team is one way to simplify the preparation process for using *MOMStories* in your follow-up group. Members of your group can share the responsibility for these tasks by individually reading Scripture for the upcoming Sunday from their Bibles or from *At Home with the Word* and the appropriate MOMStory for that Sunday (see pages 66–67 for Index of Weekly Scripture Readings: Cycle B).

- **Presenter:** Assign Scripture reading ahead of your session so that everyone comes prepared to share her thoughts. Set up expectations that each participant come having already read the materials and answered the questions that accompany the week's MOMStory.

- **Facilitator Team:** Gather fifteen minutes before the scheduled starting time for last-minute room preparations, name tags, music, etc. Be sure you start and end on time.

- **Prayer Leader:** Light the Christ candle. Have a few minutes of silence and lead the group in saying a gathering prayer.

- **Guardian Angel:** Invite each woman to share any "grace-filled" event, situation, or insight since the last meeting.

- **Presenter:** Have participants read the Scripture for the Sunday to be discussed and invite anyone in the group to share her thoughts on what the passage meant in her life.

- **Guardian Angel:** Read from *MOMStories* for the same Sunday, inviting the sharing process to continue.

- **Presenter:** Read the discussion questions one at a time. Go around the group, inviting each person to share her answers.

- **Guardian Angel:** Alert the group when there are only ten minutes left in the session.

- **Prayer Leader:** Play quiet music to set a meditative or reflective tone, inviting each woman to pray for the grace to integrate Scripture and Christ's life into her own "mom story."

- **Guardian Angel:** Remind the entire group of the time and place where you will meet and of the assigned readings.

- **Facilitator Team:** If everyone has not received a copy of the "Group Rules for Ongoing Groups" (on the next page), make certain each person receives a copy. Be sure the leaders model the Group Rules in their behavior. When participants do not follow these rules, the group can easily lose its focus.

For copies of *At Home With The Word* call (800) 933-1800 or fax (800) 933-7094.

Group Rules for Ongoing Groups

- **Punctuality:** Start and end on time. I will be punctual.

- **Anonymity:** I will not reveal what someone else has personally shared in the group with anyone outside the group.

- **Respect and Trust:** I will respect the right of each person to have her own thoughts, feelings, and beliefs based on her knowledge and life experience. I will trust that my dignity and life experience will be respected as well.

- **Non-Judgment:** I will not judge others. Feelings are not right or wrong. Each person has unique, valuable life experiences.

- **Gentleness:** I will be kind and gentle with myself and others. Hurting persons tend to reach out and hurt other persons. Healing persons tend to reach out with healing compassion.

- **Listening:** I will listen attentively and will not interrupt when another person is talking.

- **Sharing:** I will focus on my true self and try to use first person (I, me, myself) in my conversation. I give myself the freedom to share or pass. I will allow time for each person to share.

- **Rescuing:** I will not preach, editorialize, give advice, or try to problem-solve and/or rescue others. Each person has an ability to solve her own problems.

- **Cross-Talk and Interruptions:** I will not laugh at someone who is talking. I will not talk to others during another person's sharing. I will not interrupt.

- **Mutual Responsibility:** As the group continues to meet, I will take my turn as facilitator. Leadership rotates among the members; this allows me to strengthen my facilitator/leadership skills at my own pace.

Index of Themes

Index of Weekly Scripture Readings: Cycle B

Sunday/Feast	1st Reading	Psalm	2nd Reading	Gospel	Page
Ascension	Acts 1:1–11	47	Eph 1:17–23	Mk 16:15–20	31
7th Easter	Acts 1:15–17	103	1 Jn 4:11–16	Jn 17:11b–19	32
Pentecost	Acts 2:1–11	104	1 Cor 12:3b–7,12–13	Jn 20:19–23	33
Trinity Sunday	Dt 4:32–34,39–40	33	Rom 8:14–17	Mt 28:16–20	34
Corpus Christi	Ex 24:3–8	116	Heb 9:11–15	Mk 14:12–16,22–26	35
13th Ordinary	Wis 1:13–15; 2:23–24	30	2 Cor 8:7,9,13–15	Mk 5:21–43	36
14th Ordinary	Ez 2:2–5	123	2 Cor 12:7–10	Mk 6:1–6	37
15th Ordinary	Am 7:12–15	85	Eph 1:3–14	Mk 6:7–13	38
16th Ordinary	Jer 23:1–6	23	Eph 2:13–18	Mk 6:30–34	39
17th Ordinary	2Kgs 4:42–44	145	Eph 4:1–6	Jn 6:1–15	40
Transfiguration	Dn 7:9–10,13–14	97	2 Pt 1:16–19	Mk 9:2–10	41
19th Ordinary	1 Kgs 19:4–8	34	Eph 4:30—5:2	Jn 6:41–51	42
20th Ordinary	Prv 9:1–6	34	Eph 5:15–20	Jn 6:51–58	43
21st Ordinary	Jos 24:1–2a,15–17,18b	34	Eph 5:21–32	Jn 6:60–69	44
22nd Ordinary	Dt 4:1–2,6–8	15	Jas 1:17–18,21b–22,27	Mk 7:1–8,14–15, 21–23	45
23rd Ordinary	Is 35:4–7a	146	Jas 2:1–5	Mk 7:31–37	46
24th Ordinary	Is 50:4c–9a	116	Jas 2:14–18	Mk 8:27–35	47
25th Ordinary	Wis 2:12,17–20	54	Jas 3:16–4:3	Mk 9:30–37	48
26th Ordinary	Nm 11:25–29	19	Jas 5:1–6	Mk 9:38–43,45, 47–48	49
27th Ordinary	Gn 2:18–24	128	Heb 2:9–11	Mk 10:2–16	50
28th Ordinary	Wis 7:7–11	90	Heb 4:12–13	Mk 10:17–30	51
29th Ordinary	Is 53:10–11	33	Heb 4:14–16	Mk 10:35–45	52
30th Ordinary	Jer 31:7–9	126	Heb 5:1–6	Mk 10:46–52	53
31st Ordinary	Dt 6:2–6	18	Heb 7:23–28	Mk 12:28b–34	54
32nd Ordinary	1 Kgs 17:10–16	146	Heb 9:24–28	Mk 12:38–44	55
33rd Ordinary	Dn 12:1–3	16	Heb 10:11–14,18	Mk 13:24–32	56
Christ the King	Dn 7:13–14	93	Rv 1:5–8	Jn 18:33b–37	57

More Resources for MOMS

MOMS
A Personal Journal
Paula Hagen with Vickie LoPiccolo Jennett
Paper, 144 pages, 7" x 10", 0-89390-224-1

Use these reflections to look at your values, the choices you make each day, and to ponder the love you share with others in your life. The Personal Journal is used as the basis for a beginning MOMS group.

MOMS
Developing a Ministry
Paula Hagen and Patricia Hoyt
Paper, 132 pages, 8 1/2" x 11", 0-89390-368-X

This newly revised and comprehensive manual is filled with resources and guidelines for setting up the Ministry of Mothers Sharing (MOMS) program within any church community. It includes detailed lesson plans, job desciptions for leaders, administrative and publicity procedures and other reproducible handouts tht will make implementing your program a breeze.

MOMS
Facilitator's Guide
Paula Hagen, Vickie LoPiccolo Jennett, and Patricia Hoyt
Paper, 144 pages, 8 1/2" x 11", 0-89390-256-X

This revised edition of the Facilitator's Guide includes everything both the first-time and seasoned facilitator need to lead a MOMS support group.

More Resources for MOMS

MOMStories
Instant Inspiration for Mothers
Vicki LoPiccolo Jennett with reflection questions by Paula Hagen
Paper, 80 pages, 5 1/2" x 8 1/2", 0-89390-445-7

The original MOMStories has down-earth stories that you'll recognize as your own. Includes an index linking the stories to the lectionary (Cycle A).

A Prayer Companion for MOMS
Vickie LoPiccolo Jennett with Paula Hagen
Paper, 104 pages, 4"x6", 0-89390-265-9

This purse-size book is for all women who recognize a dimension of the spirituality found in the challenges and joys of motherhood. The authors offer reflections on such everyday experiences as juggling schedules, cleaning the refrigerator, waiting in line, and taking time out for fun. Keep a pen handy, too, because there's space for you to write your own thoughts and feelings.

AT-HOME MOTHERHOOD
Making It Work for You
Cindy Tolliver
Paper, $14.95, 152 pages, 6"x9", 0-89390-295-0

In a career-oriented world, staying at home to be a full-time parent presents new as well old challenges. Cindy Tolliver examines at-home motherhood as a valid choice for sophisticated women - and shows you how to make the most of it. For yourself, your family, and your community.

Order these books from your local bookseller or call:
1-888-273-7782 (toll-free) or 1-408-286-8505.
Visit our website at www.pinet.com